How to Draw FUNNY FACES

Illustrated by
Karen Walker and Georgene Griffin

Incorporated

Copyright © 1997 Kidsbooks Inc.
3535 West Peterson Avenue
Chicago, IL 60659

INTRODUCTION

This book will show you how to draw lots of different funny faces. Some are more difficult than others, but if you follow along, step-by-step, you'll soon be able to draw any funny face you wish.

SUPPLIES

NUMBER 2 PENCILS   FELT-TIP PEN
SOFT ERASER   COLORED PENCILS,
DRAWING PAD   MARKERS, OR CRAYONS

Each funny face in this book begins with several basic shapes, usually a combination of circles and ovals. Many variations of these shapes, along with other lines, will also be used.

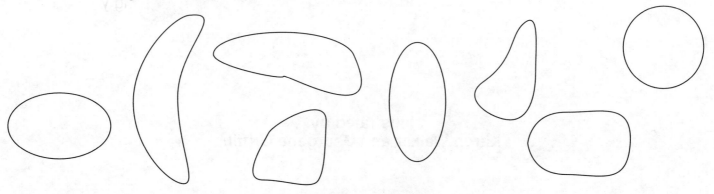

HELPFUL HINTS

1. In the first two steps of each drawing you will create a solid foundation of the figure—much like a builder who must first construct a foundation before building the rest of the house. Next comes the fun part—creating the smooth, clean drawing of the funny face, and adding all the finishing touches—details, shading, and color.

Following the first two steps carefully will make the final steps easier.

2. Always keep your pencil lines light and soft. These "guide-lines" will be easier to erase when you no longer need them.

3. Don't be afraid to erase. It usually takes a lot of drawing a erasing before you are satisfied with the way your drawing looks. Each funny face has special characteristics that make easier, or in some cases, harder to draw. However, it is easie to draw anything if you break it down into simple shapes.

4. Add details and all the finishing touches after you have blended and refined all the shapes and your funny face is complete.

5. Remember: Practice makes perfect. Don't be discouraged you can't get the hang of it right away. Just keep drawing and erasing until you do.

HOW TO START

Begin by drawing basic shapes—ovals and a rectangle for ● general outline of the head like the one on this page.

Add the other shapes to the first ones. These are the basic ●idelines that form the funny face and create the foundation. ●e dotted lines show what can be erased as you go along.

●MEMBER TO KEEP YOUR LINES LIGHTLY DRAWN

●Carefully create the final shape of the face as you add the ●aracteristics that make the face funny. Keep erasing any ●idelines you no longer need as you go along. Finally, blend ● various shapes and forms so your drawing looks smooth.

4. Continue to refine your drawing as you add shading, other details, and the finishing touches. When your funny face is complete, color it with your favorite colors or, for a more dramatic effect, outline it with a thick, black marker.

5. Use your imagination and feel free to create details other than the ones shown. You may even want to add backgrounds to enhance your drawings. When you have drawn some or all of the funny faces in this book, and are comfortable with your drawing technique, start creating your own.

Most of all, **HAVE FUN!**

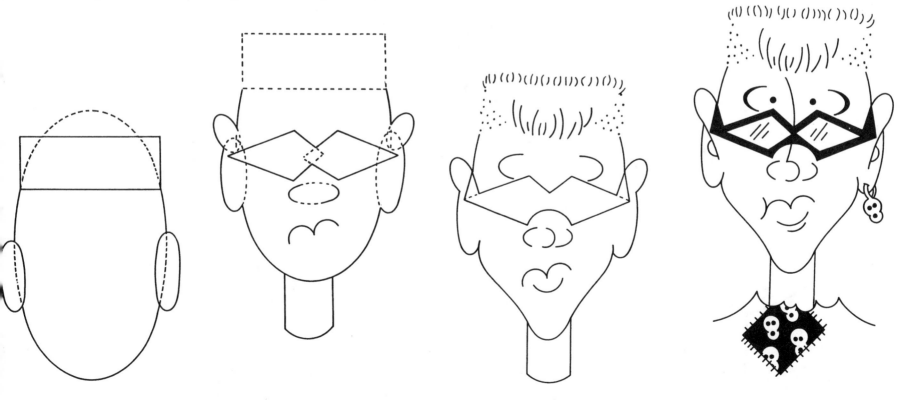

Zany Zack

1. Lightly draw a large circle for the head and smaller circles for the ears, eyes, and mouth. Add a small square for the neck.

Note: All the guide-lines in steps 1 and 2 should always be lightly drawn. If you don't like the way something looks, erase and try again.

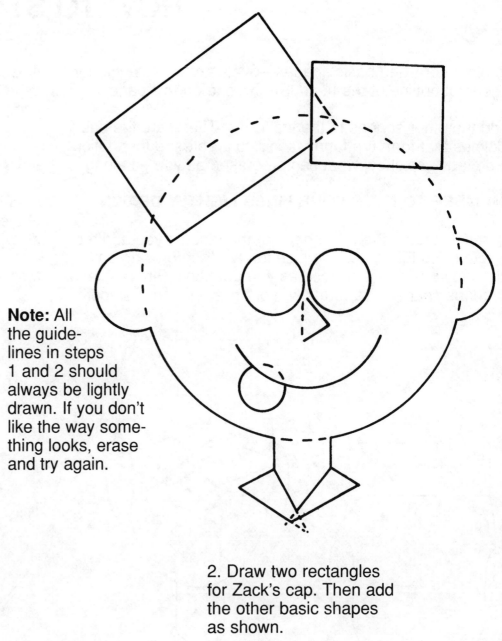

2. Draw two rectangles for Zack's cap. Then add the other basic shapes as shown.

3. Add two smaller circles for Zany Zack's pupils. Then draw his bushy hair with a squiggly line. Curve and blend the rectangular lines to form his cap.

Remember, feel free to change one or more features. Add your own details, shading, or colors. What you see here and on the following pages is simply a guide to help you get started.

4. Use your imagination. Add polka dots, freckles, and other details to make Zany Zack look zanier than ever!

Nerdy Natalie

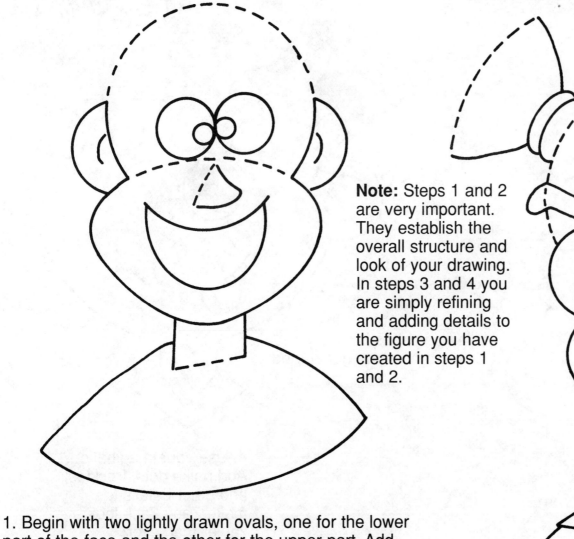

Note: Steps 1 and 2 are very important. They establish the overall structure and look of your drawing. In steps 3 and 4 you are simply refining and adding details to the figure you have created in steps 1 and 2.

1. Begin with two lightly drawn ovals, one for the lower part of the face and the other for the upper part. Add the guideline circles for the eyes and pupils, and the simple shapes for the nose, mouth, and ears. Then draw the lines for the neck and blouse.

3. Draw the outline of Natalie's hair with a wavy line, erasing any guidelines you no longer need as you go along. Add the teeth, and when you're satisfied with the way your picture looks, start adding the finishing touches.

4. Complete Nerdy Natalie by using your imagination and adding any details or colors you wish.

Funky Fred

Hint: Always begin by drawing the largest shape first.

1. Sketch a large oval for the head. Then add two small ovals for the ears, and a rectangle to use as a guide for Fred's funky hair.

2. Draw the additional guideline shapes: intersecting diamonds for the glasses, small ovals for the tops of his ears, and a small oval for his nose. Finally, add the neck and a curved line for his mouth.

3. Shape the bottom part of Fred's face as shown. Then fill in his hair with lines and dots. Add half circles for the eyes, tip of the nose, and his bottom lip. Erase any unneeded guidelines as you continue to refine your picture.

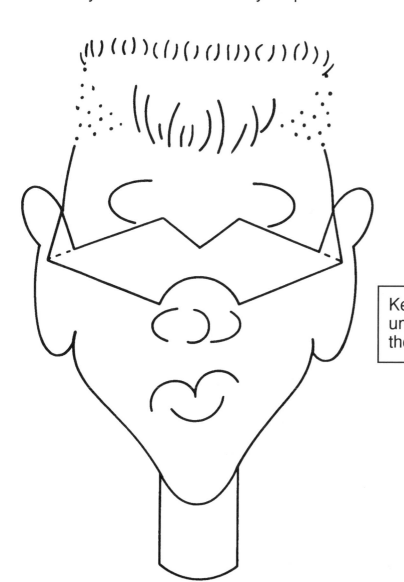

Keep drawing and erasing until you are satisfied with the way your picture looks.

4. Now make Funky Fred even funkier. Add shading, an earring, a shirt collar, and anything else that's fun.

Puckering Penelope

2. Carefully draw the lines that form the brim of her hat. Then add a row of small ovals for the hair. Add her pupils, and if you like, some freckles.

1. Start by lightly sketching a large, free-form guideline shape for Penelope's face. Add circles for her ears and two overlapping ovals for her eyes. Continue adding the simple shapes for her nose, lips, and neck.

Remember: Practice makes perfect. Keep drawing and erasing until you are satisfied with the way your picture looks.

3. Blend and refine all the lines and shapes together. Add Penelope's eyelids and lashes. Draw two strings of tiny circles and a heart to form her necklace, and add a top and some flowers to her hat.

4. For the finishing touches, add extra details as shown, especially the highlights on Penelope's puckered lips.

Steaming Stan

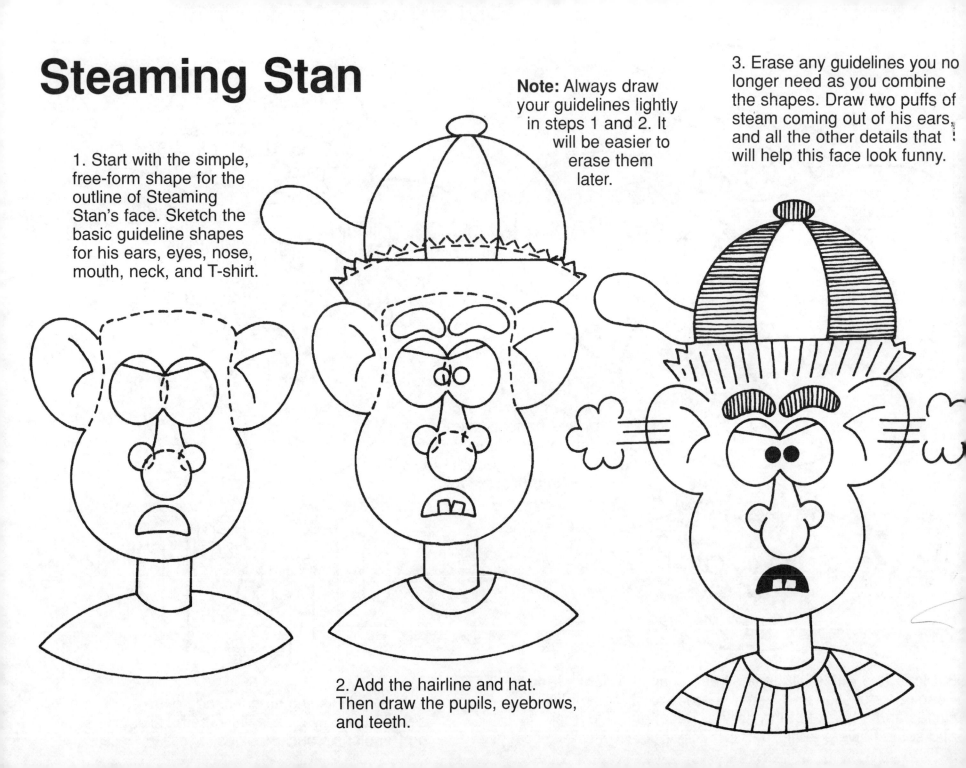

Note: Always draw your guidelines lightly in steps 1 and 2. It will be easier to erase them later.

1. Start with the simple, free-form shape for the outline of Steaming Stan's face. Sketch the basic guideline shapes for his ears, eyes, nose, mouth, neck, and T-shirt.

2. Add the hairline and hat. Then draw the pupils, eyebrows, and teeth.

3. Erase any guidelines you no longer need as you combine the shapes. Draw two puffs of steam coming out of his ears, and all the other details that will help this face look funny.

Star-Spangled Granny

1. Form Granny's head and hair with ovals and a rectangle. Add small squares for her eyeglasses, and a circle for her nose.

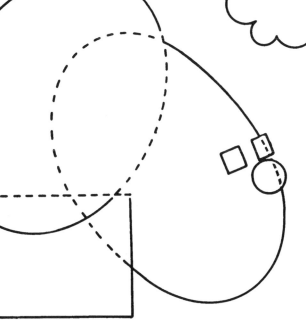

2. Draw the headband guidelines and curve Granny's hair with a wavy line all around her head as shown. Her necklace and earring are formed with little circles. Round out the face, lips, and chin.

3. Add details like Granny's headband bow and stars, and curved mouth. Then add shading. Now Granny is set for a star-spangled celebration.

Ms. Head O'Hair

1. Lightly draw a large circle guide-line for the outer hairline. Add other circles for the face, eyes, and ears. Draw an oval for the nose.

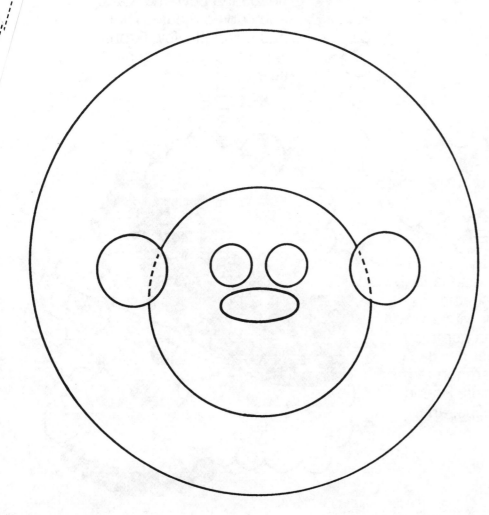

2. Create the hair by drawing lots of little curves around the outer guideline circle. Add the tiny pupils, a half circle for the mouth, and the neck.

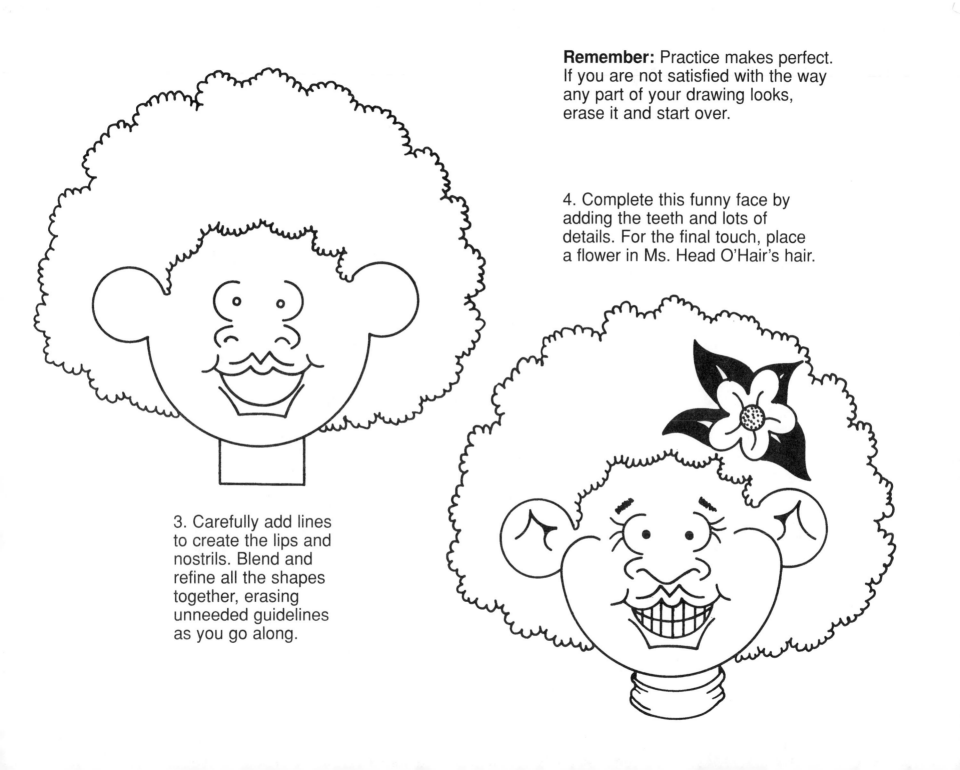

Remember: Practice makes perfect. If you are not satisfied with the way any part of your drawing looks, erase it and start over.

4. Complete this funny face by adding the teeth and lots of details. For the final touch, place a flower in Ms. Head O'Hair's hair.

3. Carefully add lines to create the lips and nostrils. Blend and refine all the shapes together, erasing unneeded guidelines as you go along.

Wendy Weirdo

1. Begin by drawing an oval guideline shape for the head. Add the other basic shapes for the ears, eyes, nose, and upper part of her hair.

2. Add the neck and collar. Then sketch the curvy lines for the mouth and lips. Next, add the glasses, and lastly, her headband and the lower part of her hair.

Remember: Keep all your lines lightly drawn until you get to the final stages.

This drawing may look difficult, but it's easy to draw almost anything if you break it down into simple shapes.

3. Erase the unneeded guidelines as you blend the lines and shapes into a smooth, finished drawing. Add earrings and a star on her headband, then go on to the final stage.

4. Add shading and other details as shown to complete your drawing of Wendy Weirdo. When you're done, color her hair, glasses, and collar with some weird colors.

Hokey Hal

Note: It's usually easier to begin any drawing by sketching the largest shape first.

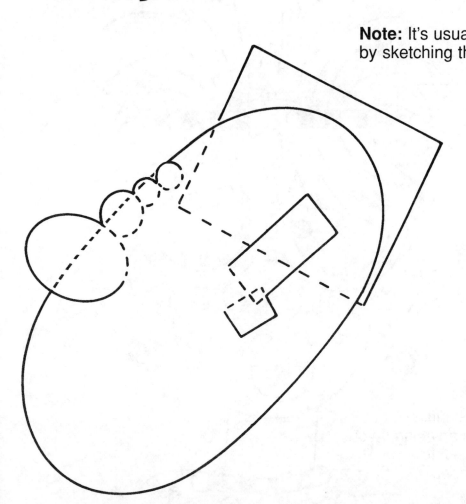

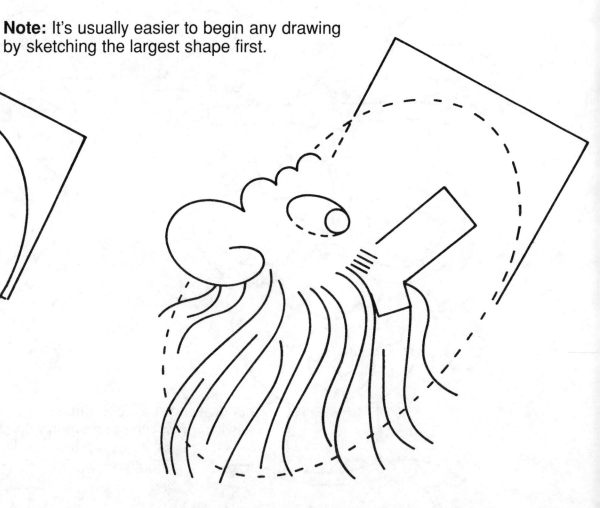

1. Begin your drawing with a large oval guide-line shape for the head and a square for the top of the hat. Add three circles and an oval for the nose, and two rectangles for the ear.

2. Blend the nose shapes together and curl the oval to form the nostril. Create the eye. Then draw long, wavy lines for the beard.

3. Add an oval for the front brim of the hat and a half-moon to form the back brim. Erase any guidelines you no longer need.

4. To complete Hokey Hal, add shading, details, and a fine flower to his hat.

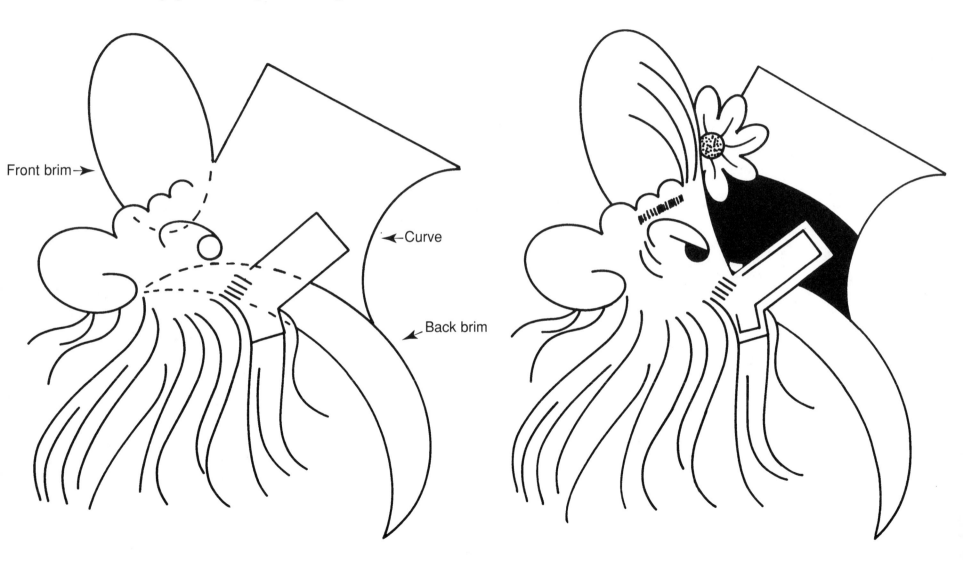

Front brim→

←Curve

Back brim

Laughing Larry

2. Draw Larry's hair with continuous curved lines. Then add the pupils, eyelids, eyebrows, teeth, and tongue. Finally, add a waving tie to his collar.

1. Lightly draw the outline of Larry's curly hair. Then draw the outline of his face and the guideline shapes for eyes, nose, mouth, and ear.

3. Now add all the finishing touches. Darken the pupils and the inside of the mouth, and add polka dots to his tie. What other details would you like to add?

Goofy Gil

1. Start with a lightly drawn oval for the head. Create the eyes, ears, and mouth with circles. Add a triangle shape for his nose and a small rectangle for his neck.

2. Sketch some long curved lines for his hair and shoulders, and two ovals for the collar. Erase any unneeded lines as you start defining your picture.

3. To complete this funny face, add the mouth, some shading, and other details as shown.

Tear On Perforated Line

Silly Sue

Note: Always draw your guidelines lightly in steps 1 and 2. It will be easier to erase them later.

1. Start by sketching guideline circles for the head, hair, eyes, and ears as shown. Add an oval for her bangs.

2. Draw wavy lines around the outer circle, forming Sue's hair. Next, add a three-leaf clover for her nose, and the other basic shapes as shown.

3. Add eyelids, jagged lines to form the bangs, and two small half-ovals for the nostrils. Round and curve the lips and mouth, erasing any lines you no longer need.

4. Complete the collar. Then add eyelashes, earrings, shading, and any other details that will make Silly Sue look as silly as possible.

Dejected Jake

2. Carefully add the brim of the hat. Draw the curved lines to form the hair, and lastly, the neck, shoulder, and bandanna.

1. Lightly draw a free-form oval for the basic head shape. Add the other simple shapes for the ears, eyes, nose, and curved mouth.

Note: Steps 1 and 2 establish the overall structure and look of your drawing. In steps 3 and 4 you are simply refining and adding details.

3. Blend and refine all the shapes. Erase any unnecessary lines. When you're satisfied with the way your drawing looks, add a single tooth, a top to Jake's hat, and a few playing cards.

4. For the finishing touches add a checkered pattern to Dejected Jake's bandanna and to the ribbon on his hat. Add shading and any other details you wish.

Screamin' Mimi

1. Begin with three lightly drawn, large ovals. Remember to draw the largest one first.

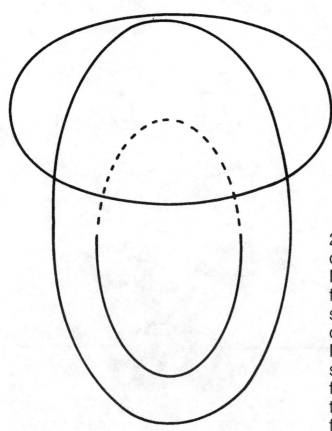

2. Draw the five small connecting circles for Mimi's hair bow, and form her hair. Draw a straight line through the center oval to form Mimi's mouth, and a small square guideline for her teeth. Then add the other basic shapes for her neck and collar.

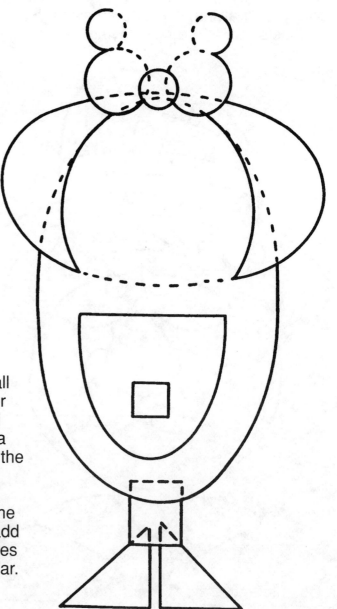

4. Add glasses and the remaining details as shown. Then add some shading and get a real scream out of Mimi!

Note: Keep erasing unneeded guidelines and redrawing any parts of your picture that you're not satisfied with. When you feel it looks "just right" start adding the finishing touches.

3. Complete the hair bow and add the eyes, nose, and earrings. Add overlapping triangles for her upper lip and complete the mouth as shown.

Smilin' Satch

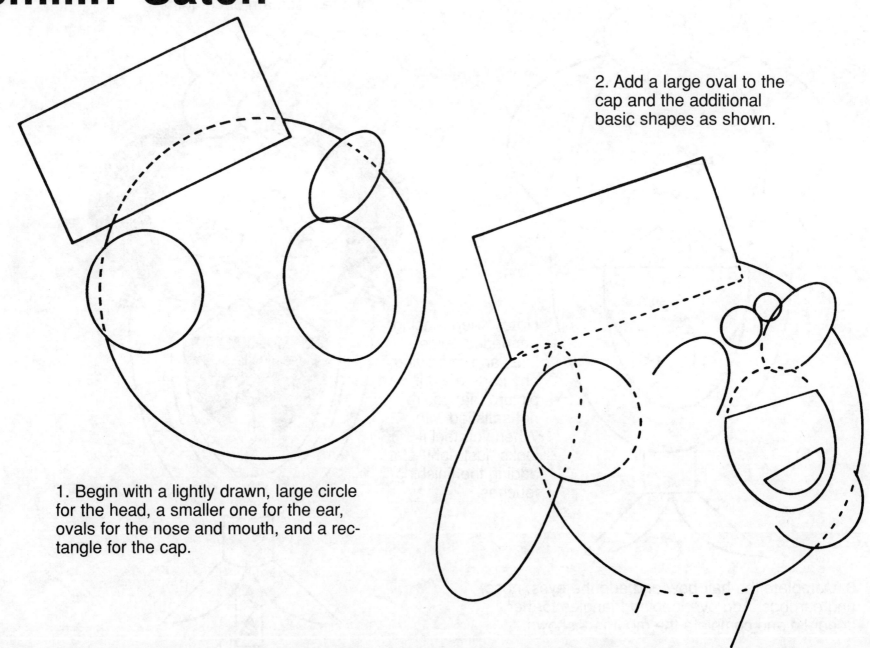

1. Begin with a lightly drawn, large circle for the head, a smaller one for the ear, ovals for the nose and mouth, and a rectangle for the cap.

2. Add a large oval to the cap and the additional basic shapes as shown.

3. Draw jagged lines for Satch's hair, two small circles for his pupils, two tiny square teeth, and his tongue. Then round and refine all the lines on Satch's hat. Note the opening where his hair pops through. Erase any lines you no longer need as you curve, connect, and blend all these shapes together.

4. Add all the extra details and shading to complete your picture of Smilin' Satch. Here's one funny face you won't forget!

Stern-faced Sophie

2. Draw the hat, and add a ribbon and flower to it. Add guidelines for her hair, and add another flower on the ribbon around her neck.

Note: Guidelines should always be lightly drawn. If you don't like the way something looks, erase and try again.

1. Lightly sketch a free-form circle for the head. Then, taking one feature at a time, carefully draw the guideline shapes for the ears, eyes, glasses, nose, and lips. Then add the neck, shoulder, and ribbon.

4. Finish Sophie's funny face by adding details and shading to the ribbons and flowers.

3. Blend and refine all the shapes and lines into a smooth outline drawing of Stern-faced Sophie. Erase unneeded guidelines as you go along.

Pigeon-head Pete

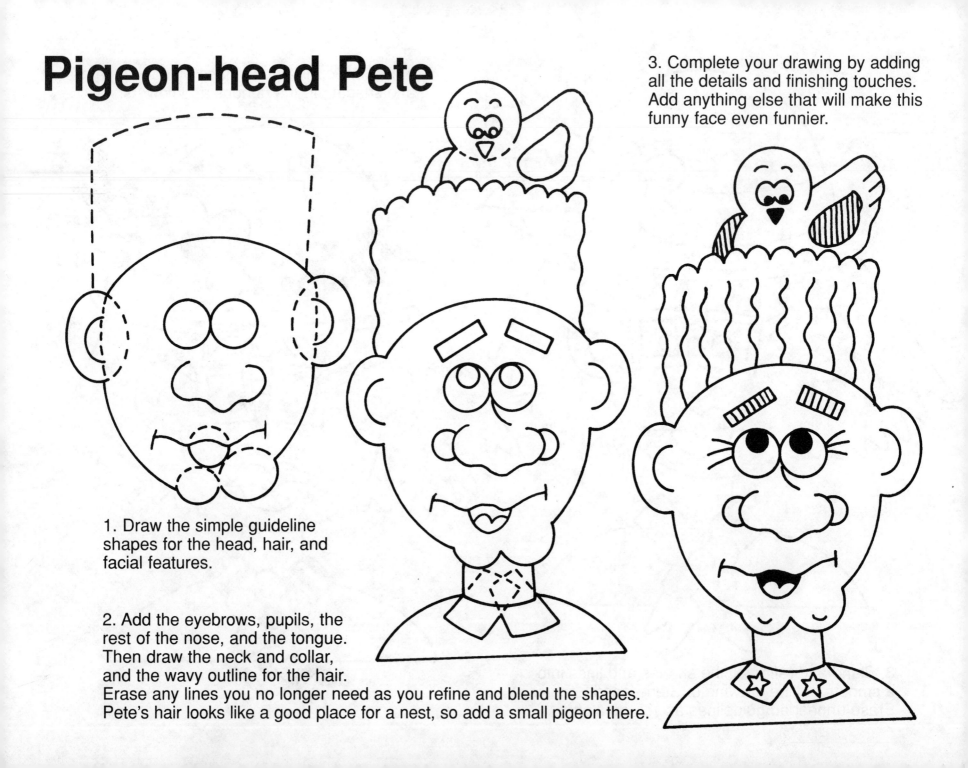

3. Complete your drawing by adding all the details and finishing touches. Add anything else that will make this funny face even funnier.

1. Draw the simple guideline shapes for the head, hair, and facial features.

2. Add the eyebrows, pupils, the rest of the nose, and the tongue. Then draw the neck and collar, and the wavy outline for the hair. Erase any lines you no longer need as you refine and blend the shapes. Pete's hair looks like a good place for a nest, so add a small pigeon there.